I0141635

BARLOW UNBOUND

BARLOW UNBOUND

A vulgar trip into the mock heroic:
an entertainment
from the years after the Second World War.

Keith Howden

PENNILESS PRESS PUBLICATIONS

Published by

Penniless Press Publications April 2022

Keith Howden

The author asserts his moral right to be identified as the author of the work. All rights reserved. No part of this publication may be reproduced, stored in a retrieval system or transmitted in any form or by any means, electronic, mechanical, photocopying, recording or otherwise, without the prior permission of the publishers.

ISBN 978-1-913144-36-4

Contents

Barlow Unbound

The *lines* of James Bird Horobin

An essay upon the *lines* of James Bird Horobin

Because of a certain expertise I have previously shown in such matters, I was asked by the *Phaeton Poetry Society* to provide as best I might, a 'translation' and an honest explanation of these *documents*. I have hesitated to call them poems, as did the writer himself. In a manuscript outside the works here presented, he denies the existence of 'poetry' in his work and further than that, denies even the classification of his oeuvre, as verse, preferring instead the title of *lines*. The reason that he gives for this I have perused in a heavily creased and incomplete missive cum manifesto that he apparently wrote to a friend. In it, he writes pretentiously that he is seeking a language that can accommodate all emotions and styles. This language he says, may come from the invisible part between two expressions of the same event which can create a multiple *compression*. I do not know what he means. He further claims that such writing must accommodate in a both backward and forward movement the banal with the meaningful, the pathetic with the bathetic, the crude with the refined, the sentimental with the incisive. The list he draws up, in some sort of attempt to protect himself, is both mirth provoking and apparently endless. Subsequent pages are wholly written in what might be conceived as a deliberate masking or shielding of their content, frequently in a kind of code that records with obscuring care only their sounds, and these same sounds in their uttering conceived originally in a dialect that would not be easily understood by the general reader. I am again uncertain of his meaning.

The manuscripts, such as they are, untidy and out of order, were discovered in the attics of a house previously occupied by James Bird Horobin. My approach to the translation of Horobin's *code* (though that might suggest a system more complex than was actually the case) was greatly aided by the discovery, at the same time, of a tape recording on a very early machine of that type, and of three reasonably large sections of the works. Only by comparing the coded sounds of the manuscripts with the dialect sound of the recordings, was I able to extract a sufficient understanding of what Horobin had presumably intended. It is through these two aids that I have fashioned the instruments by which I have endeavoured to construct a language which might make them available, should he so wish, to the 'common' reader

Others have seen fit to examine and assess these pieces as a kind of primitive poetry and worth some attention. Also, there have been other attempts at translation of the *lines* but they are regarded as unsatisfactory since no previous assessor of the work had either the opportunity or the material of both written and recorded examples to work with. I think these examples, despite their plurality might well be what I have come to call my 'Rosetta Stone.'

I have been, and I must acknowledge the fact, more than a little disappointed. The *lines* are coarse and rough: their language is frequently indelicate and their structures are often far from the necessarily harmonious construction that I expect poetry (even when it is merely denoted as *lines*) to deliver. There is none of that necessary delicacy of poetry within them. They are not poetry as I was taught to understand it in my schooldays. The clearest handwriting, where it occasionally occurs, is that of an uneducated man, though there is, I believe, some evidence of self-education. My work as an Accounts Clerk over many years has taught me to estimate, usually quite correctly, both character and intelligence as handwriting absorbs and displays it. I have had need, throughout my consideration and lengthy correction (perhaps even creation) of these texts, to deal with a form of spelling (among the few clearly written artefacts) that is, to say the least, rudimentary.

James Bird Horobin is not provably their author's name (though I have little doubt that that must be the case) since where questions of their creation and creator arise either within or accompanying the texts, they are claimed by pseudonym to be the work of either *Mad* or *Daft Jack.* Without final proof, I am inclined to believe that the two titles refer to the same individual. There is some possibility that Horobin, in his youth, had been variously known as either *Mad* or *Daft* Jack, though the evidence is insubstantial and lies in hearsay more than in fact. There are other records, perhaps more substantial, of his frequent youthful misbehaviour and misdeeds: There is also later evidence that he spent some time under strict confinement in a mental establishment though I have not been able to discover the precise aspects of or causes for this. At other times, I have been led to believe, although the evidence is yet again fragmentary, that if indeed the author of the present material is Horobin, he produced two small self-published documents. One of these was believed to have been called *Daft Jack's Ideal Republics* and the other, *Natural Fascism.* No copy of these works is available and because of their likely quality and their mode of production, it is unlikely that either was reviewed or even taken seriously. In these *lines* under consideration, Horobin recounts what seem to be three salient events of his youth. Perhaps his way of life, which I am led to believe was rough, could only be recounted by what I feel is an accompanying and unnecessary roughness of thought. Moral delicacy has no place in the works. In particular, I found both the language and the morality of those scenes of a sexual nature, even within the context of an attempted accuracy, to be both distasteful and disturbing.

It needs to be said here that although I have frequently aspired to express my deepest feelings in verse, I am not a man of any literary erudition. There was little gentility in the manner I was given education and at best, poetry was a side-issue for those more gifted and more intended for another dimension of education than I myself was or could afford to be at that time. I was, of course, taught to respect and recognize those aspects of language and shape to which poetry ought properly to conform in order to be spiritually effective. There are, in my 'translation,' as I point out above, certain scenes and descriptions of a sexual nature which are graphic enough to be offensive to a more cultured taste, but in my defence, I would argue that it is the translator's lot to be true to the spirit of the work before him however distasteful he might find it. On this point perhaps, I need to apologise for allowing such unpleasantness to remain in my translation, but with some revulsion, I needed to be true to the task that I had set myself.

I shall remain anonymous though I would prefer it to be known that I have always considered myself to be a gentleman. I have refined table manners and in age speak more correctly and in a better accent than the one I inherited. My work, to the best of my knowledge has always been carefully correct. My employers have frequently applauded my modest achievements and occasionally I have been rewarded with the type of commendation which tends to bespeak my professional responsibility and reliability. I do however recognize that I am not necessarily well-qualified to undertake the task which, by chance, has befallen me in this present work.

Horobin's work seems to deal only with personal experience. He rarely attempts, and has little capacity to move away from the self and the mundane into those higher realms that, it seems to me, true poetry should demand. And, of course, even with his evasion excuse of *lines* he should not escape those conditions that poetry, by its nature demands. His obsession with what he calls 'the rendering of experience' is manifested in repetitions and circumlocution, to meet his belief that the 'truth' of any event can only be rendered by approaching the act from different perspectives and angles. This apparently sophisticated belief in an author so manifestly coarse and simple, I find somewhat surprising. Certainly it is a mode by which a trained and experienced mind might seek to render experience, though that in itself suggests to me that it is not the kind of immediate truth that poetry at its best should seek. Poetry, I feel, should strongly convey the truthful, the moral and the beautiful. Horobin's work contains no awareness of and indeed no recognition of such demands. Perhaps, sadly, the most literate parts of his oeuvre are those quotations he uses from the relatively low journalism which occurred in the *Bugle,* a local weekly newspaper of that post-war time now happily defunct. *The Bugle* was never allowed to enter my home household since it was considered to be cheap and tasteless, a model of unacceptable writing, *the academy of journalese* as my father used to call it. It was variously reputed to be frequently untruthful, to be in hock with the local tradesmen and shopkeepers whose advertisements adorned so many of its pages and generally a poor influence on a growing boy's mind. Readers of its pages, my father used to say, were paving their own way to a benighted existence, although I suppose it is only fair to mention that he had quarrelled with many of its advertisers, its subscribers and even members of its management during the period of the failure of his own small business. It was after his death that mother and I moved to the somewhat lower status of our subsequent dwelling. I should note here that printed matter of all sorts was a consistent subject of debate in our household. I was once punished quite heavily when my father discovered that I had brought home two copies of comics, the *Dandy* and *Beano* loaned to me by some fellow classmate in what might have been a moment of pity. It was made plain to me that these were not materials that he believed suitable reading for a child of my years and that I should immerse myself in more profitable speculation and the sort of literature that recommended more thoughtful hobbies and pursuits since that was the way to get on in life. Consequently, I spent much of my childhood and younger years learning to sit in postures to make myself appear both usefully alert and interested in material that was not to my taste and often almost wholly outside my interests and capabilities. These were the dreadful days of *The Boys Own Paper* and Arthur Mee's *Children's Encyclopaedia* which were obtained and thrust before me to be my guides to a more prosperous future. I had no desire to build a working model lighthouse as my monthly project: (what could it possibly do apart from show a light?): I did not want to become expert in the management and accumulation of toy railway stock or in the games and rules of rugby football and cricket which were as far outside my understanding as the language and behaviour of the Public Schools whose world they were meant to convey. What was the *Remove?* A concept of which I had no understanding. I had no experience of the forms of fellowship that such exertions and institutions seemed to encourage. I could go on in a similar fashion about the world presented to me in the *Encyclopaedia.* But suffice to say that cold statuary and a dulling moral content did little to unfreeze my world. I was a lonely child and a friendless youth. My escape was to find satisfaction in both reading and creating, within my limited knowledge and education, the kinds of poetry that succeed in promoting the good and the moral and fulfil the highest expectations of human achievement.

Mr Horobin's *lines*, for me, fulfil neither the conditions of his manifesto nor do they achieve that *compression* which he supposes intensifies meaning.

From *The Bugle*.

'William _____ had volunteered for Army Service in 1940 and had seen action in both Italy and Germany. He had, Counsel said, found it difficult to readjust to civilian life and had come to believe that his wife had been consistently unfaithful to him during his absence. These suspicions, though members of the Jury might find them risible had their consequences not been so terrible, he had based on the evidence of a budgerigar, or perhaps a parrot, persistently repeating the names of her supposed lovers and of the presumed father of his wife's child. In a fit of jealous rage, he had strangled his wife......'

A Birdseed Symphony

1. Piano Tom

Then up she gets, that pissed Terpsichore,
snake from a basket, swiping brown ale
and bottles of stout, a spit trail's slurry
slugging her lipstick and chin. *Seen it before, girl,*
last week at the Alhambra, this was on the bill.

Starts to blabber nonsense, shouts she's Salome,
shaking her tits at closing time in the bar.
Spit lengthened, swung on her chin. *Salome*
was last week's offering at the Alhambra.
Tonight, whose bloody head hedgehogs the platter?

God, she was terrible to watch, my Salome.
That crazed look, that string of spit and snot
gilding her chin, dancing through scummy
Guinness and broken bottles. *This was last week's tit*
at the Alhambra. I queued to see it.

And then she fell. I flapped the *Woodbines*
poster over her lipstick and slugged chin.
She'd started to shout about butterflies
and roses. *At the Alhambra, no mention*
of apples and rainbows. Out of her skin.

Lying flat out she squeals of flourishing,
some crap she'd dreamed up. Still, I went
on fanning. Somebody wiped the string
of spit with a beer mat, spreading a blood taint
of her lipstick. *The Alhambra was different.*

2. Barlow young

'Your Honour, yes, crap and derision,
here I come, aged eight, clogs in my hand,
face charcoal blackened. I command
the outhouse roof, abseil after a fashion,
the drainpipe to the backs. SALOME,
dancing a poster, flaps in the breeze
and innocence here dissolves.

                                This is
a beginning and ending. Below me,
under a hooded street light, commas
of my footprints punctuate damp cobbles.
I'm crawling through camouflage veils
of marigolds, wet earth and gossamers
of unrailed gardens. Then, Your Honour,
at fifteen Williams Street, amazement
possesses me where some lenient
curtains allow an illegal corridor,
a zebra stripe of lamplight falling across
wet marigolds. And what I see is this:
a teardrop cage, a budgerigar…

> *Coo-ee, I'm Jacky, I'm the one*
> *transmogrified and transubstantiated,*
> *translucent and translated, here inside*
> *where the mirror dangles over cuttlebone.*
> *Someone below me is mining Sarah's thighs*
> *in hairy heavings of adulterous bliss.*

…….twittering near a wireless
two drunkards in a photograph who stand
pregnant with future accusation,
shouldering Blackpool Tower. And again,
under this tarot snapshot, in its climactic and
orgasmic moment, a sexual progress
of astonishing vigour. Eavesdropping, I hear
these words: *Ooooh Sim.* A fly, Your Honour,
is battering the speckled nakedness

16

of a bulb where Sarah and her man
move with such strange athletic energy
that, battering the cage support, the budgie
swings madly over, bringing, like rain,
scutters of birdseed to a heaving arsehole
and to the tiled hearth. Then suddenly, in
this long prefigured, predestined moment, Sim
raises his head from self-dissolving burial
in Sarah's flesh to see my allegory skim
sliding the window-mirror's other side.
Knowing himself observed, still hard
in predatory accusation, Sim
comes dripping, threatening towards me.
Only SALOME and a street lamp's glaze
witness the retreating commas
of fleeing footsteps. Pre-ordainedly,
recognised or unrecognised, this augurs
the birthday of an intimacy of lives,
a collision of doppelgangers…..

3. Sarah Lucas

Squeezed on my lipstick, pursed tight lips:
my squinting image in the reproachful roost
of Billy's photograph. His dark jacket clips
wet sand, the sea's retreating rim.
And I outstared his paper eyes where pale ink scrapes
the faded signing of his simple fist:
   together, me and Sim.

Working lads staggering summer's booze:
holiday sunburn for the pit lad's outing.
Sim swells the swank tattocs
bursting his rolled sleeve's tourniquet rim
Billy's wet flannels flap. A thirst wind's carouse
trembles the sea-front pubs. Pissed handwriting:
   together me and Sim.

With Billy away to war: my lecherous
hunger for Sim. *Comes back to me,*
our squirming in flesh's octopus
reflected in a snapshot's frame.
Comes back to me, that treacherous
pantomime of skin for Billy's eye,
    together, me and Sim.

4. Sarah Lucas

'Who crapped on Billy's photograph?' she asked.
The budgie, cuckoo-barred, in still
filaments of sunlight, cocked its head.
A caterpillar of shit slid slowly
down Billy's mirror face. The bird wiped its bill.
'It's me that's in the shit,' she said.

5. Barlow

…it's CRASH. There, standing by the wireless,
its innards bleached and stained by birdshit,
Billy's photograph stares prescient
towards me where, in friendliness,
arm hooked on Simon's or on Simeon's shoulder.
they stagger under the swaying Tower,
near the elastic sea.
                    But then, Your Honour,
ecstatically raising, moaning pleasure,
a grope-delighted leg, easing the skate
of knickers past her knees, Sally Salome shocks
Billy from his frame. He falls and breaks,
relinquishing a three times folded sheet
of newspaper where an old lipstick says,
Coiled pipes and tripes is all we are.
Beside a cracked mirror, again under
the birdcage, we wrestle octopus,
tying skin's knot for pleasure's games.
Confused about the seasons, a fly

18

batters the naked bulb. My memory
nautches SALOME, proposes traitor Sim's
wartime, adulterous subterfuge
under the swinging, birdseed-scattering cage…

6. Sarah Lucas

Ooooh Simon, I squealed, confirming
my body's apostasy. I told him *No.*
He came surpliced with words, came psalming
Billy's once infidelities, entreating me to
take him. I told him *No. Coiled pipes and tripes*
(his sermon title, cursing promiscuous flesh)
is all we are, he says. Then his hand slips
to stroke me. He hymned his religious
yearning to know me, mourned unrequited
passion, flourished some silly titbit
for Billy's eyes, whose price unposted
led to my crypt. Yes, he did say *crypt.*
I wanted him. I told him *No.* He censered
his unneeded persuasions. I told him *Yes.*
Coiled pipes and tripes, he groped,
is all we are, hand biblical under my dress.
He psalmed my altar flesh but draped
his cassock to still the cagebird's oracle,
turned his reflected passion in the mirror,
of Billy's photograph to face the wall.
Unfrocked, I kissed him *Yes.* Ripe for
communion, he cleared my altar. The spirit
moved him to relish my host, to savour
untasted wine. He praised love's instrument
that clears the spirit's path, but had, for
splayed hymnbook thighs, a better vesper
to psalm salvation, to sing flesh's anthem
possessing me. I felt his flesh tremor
apostasy, pumping his exorcism
to shuddering amen. Evangelism's juice
exploded in me. I baptized myself. *Ooooh Simon*
The cage above bounced hallelujahs

and anthem seed came trickling to pattern
buttocks uncassocked pinning me down......

7. Billy's photograph

You will never hear me. Words cannot
escape the prison glass compress
sealing my lips. Traitor ink cauterizes
my missing feet. Stray days, sun's ferret
chews my unshuttable eye: rat stars
gnaw nightly at my snapshot skin. There is
no shelter in my frame's transparencies.
I watch you tarting for your night's affairs,
see the blunt bullet lipstick in your hands,
face waiting its smear. In here, the ebb-tide
ebbs forever, the sea-front pubs collude,
forever Sim and I are friends.
There is a white gull poised immortal
over the camera: its bill is bursting through
the lampshade over the radio:
a stilled wing slices your lipstick ritual.
And you will never see. That bird's eye
condemns me eavesdropper, voyeur
prisoned to undergo the Chinese torture
of your promethean infidelity
with that buck Sim. Sleepless, I mark
the oiling of your chemical machine,
the cogs and gears of flesh. Sleepless, I learn
the donkey-engine of his butting back,
the grunt and splutter of his piston lust.
I hear your cage come up...

8. Barlow young

Your Honour, here I come, still barefoot,
still carrying my shoes where glittering commas
(the time is wartime, Billy Lucas
gone to the war) of naked feet re-punctuate

20

damp pavement. MADELEINE NUDE
at the Victoria flaps the wall.
I crawl in blackout backs and still,
beneath the lighted curtains slightly parted,
someone is possing Sarah and, still slung

from a question mark, the birdcage swings
accompaniment to the engine thrustings
of someone's back. A parrot's tongue....

Coo-ee, that child's face through the glass
is with us again. Am I really there?
or did my parrot self-invent me where
the photo glistens? Was I the crass
tongued instrument of Sarah's death? When
Billy, back from the war with bomb-burst ears

pulled faces into my mirror, who remembers
those legend words? Was it Ooooh Simon?
Was it Ooooh Simeon? I offer
only the unreliability of parrots as evidence.
The mess they make with their sense-
less tongues is almost doppelganger
equivalent to the crap we can
create wagging our own....

.....staggers to silence. Drunk in that ominous
and baying photograph, three revellers
stagger to maintain the swaying poise
of Blackpool Tower. Your Honour, here it comes:
his naked and adulterous paramour is
naming him. In passion's struggle, shaking
that peardrop cage eternally beginning
its rain of birdseed to an arching arse,
she calls him Sim. Beneath that omen bird,
Ooooh Sim, she wails, forever fixed
in that orgasmic naming. It is an ending mixed
with a beginning. I know that bastard
intimately, share his shame. His long betrayals
are mine. *Ooooh Sim,* she howls.

9. Barlow

....it's CRASH. Here come the doppelganger
transgressions of my flesh. Her daughter,
Sally of Sarah, Sally of Sim's Sarah,
Salome offspring of that wartime ardour.
...it's CRASH where prescient and clairvoyant,
her father's snapshot, that baying augur
stained by birdshit, heaves towards my future
accusatory eyeing from a drunken moment
before his fiction swelled that Sim had seeded Sally,
Sally Salome, Sally of someone's Sarah
whose pipes and tripes beneath the budgerigar
I am enjoying. Straightening, for her play,

22

a naked and delighted leg for groping's pleasure,
she shocks his tarot to the hearth. Its wreck
discloses sanguine in there, someone's lipstick
on a thrice folded sheet of newspaper,
those omen words, SALOME BARE……

10. Barlow young

Your Honour, I'm here again in that equivocal
abseil to Williams Street. SALOME NUDE
madeleines a poster. Veiled by a marigold
at number seventeen, squelching an eyeball
on a cold window pane, I'm spying
on Agnes Herod, face ecstatic, wineglass
tight to her wall. Through blackout daisies
I see the deed she hears. What I'm next seeing
is this: a chest: above an open drawer,
a tinkling pot, a leaning photograph
in which four swaying drunkards, gobs agape
are grinning holiday under the Tower.
A silver question mark suspends the jet
eardrop of a black cloth draping the cage,
to prison the voice within and camouflage
the heaving act adulterous beneath
from someone's unforgiving echo.
A fly confused about the season, batters
a bulb's nakedness where coitus
wrestles to the orgasmic, crescendo
stage of an act gargantuan, heroic
in its vigour. Sarah and her lover's arse
accordion with such energy and purpose
that, colliding with the stanchion, a hook
from which the cage depends, forsakes its stays.
The black cloth slips. An anarchic eye
observes the deed in its climactic sigh
And now she names him. Is it Simon she says?
Or is it Simeon? And what did Billy guess?
Your Honour, it's something only a bird

and Agnes Herod and myself have shared
to mark this christening confusion. Does
Ooooh Simon baptismally bestride her moan
or does *Ooooh Simeon* fiction her font? Is this
a collision of doppelgangers? Did Agnes
spill it? Or else the bird? Such confusion
of hymnbook's or poetic rapture's keen
leaks dissolutions of delight to whet
a panting eavesdropper, ear flat
against the wall of number seventeen....

11. Sarah Lucas.

'Who crapped in Billy's gob?' she said.
The budgie, secret as cuttlebone
winked. A worm of shit skated
Billy's unspeaking mouth. 'He won't –'
(beak to mirror beak the bird fenced gallant)
'believe it's a load of shit,' she said.

12. Barlow

....it's CRASH. A naked limb for passion's moment,
ecstatically straightened bursts and shatters
the tarot photograph where doppelgangers
are mustering. Soiled with a cagebird's excrement
it falls and breaks. *Ooooh Sim,* I hear.
It disgorges a tattered, disembowelled
sheet of newspaper. On it, lipstick scrawled:
Coiled pipes and tripes is all we are.
....it's CRASH. *Ooooh Simeon.* A frame's guts
disgorge a disembowelled sheet
of newspaper thrice-folded. Lipstick stains it:
on it: SALOME BARE. My counterpoint lusts
disturb a chromium question mark to seed
a riddle. *Ooooh Tom,* she squeals.
A parrot spills his seed. *Ooooh Jack*, she howls...

13. Sarah Lucas

'It's a shitty business.' She pointed
her lipstick at the cage. Shit's glacier
erected Billy's window crotch. The bird
preened to seduce the mirror,
gurgled to woo where he stabbed before.
'Shit's what he was down there,' she said.

14. Barlow

....it's CRASH. It's tantrum time. Somebody's
been lying. Sal never stayed my grope.
Nor did she call me treacherous or stop
because she wanted Tom. Her promise
raised me cocksure to have her heaving
birdseed under my lust in that cold house
where years before I saw the birdseed bounce
of her begetting, outside the mirror, watching
Sim at his Eden tricks. He possed his Sarah
while over him the question mark was
dripping ambiguities. Framed in birdshit lace,
looping his arm encompassing Sim's shoulder,
Billy the cuckold kid grins innocence's trip
beneath the Tower....

        ... ,,,,, It's CRASH. Ecstatically
straightening a naked and orgasmic leg, my Salome
shatters his frame. Splayed for old octopus, ripe
for the squelch and sealing of skin's trick
she squealed her drool for me and not for Tom.
Her Salome dance had been for me. She bared a lipstick
legend staining her arm. *Sally loves Jack.*

                  That was the way
                it was. All this baloney
            was Sally playing Salome.
         she said (or did she say?):

15. Sally Lucas

After the boozing, under the smoke, this was,
moved in me, that command, a warm wind's motion,
that sudden shifting, spawning the upward rain
of pissbed parachutes from shade, airless ground.
Dance, it said, *dance.* Came homing from some land
of butterflies and rainbows, roses, apples.
I was all dances then: Salome's, Isadora's,
all the world's strippers, teasers, belly barers.

I was an instrument of succouring, nourishing,
of favouring and flourishing. I danced
from that rich tropic I had reached beyond
our little grunt and grub. I was all time's bride,
the world's grope then. Not the dead, disinfected
puppets of ballet, rigid in white. I swung
my belly resonant as drums, thrust out tight tits,
tranced by the ancient jazz of my teeming guts.

After the smut and boozy jokes, this was,
moved through me, that command, like a second's stir
presaging thunder, when a cool, windless air
stiffens among soft elderberry flounces.
Dance, it said, *dance.* I was all the world's dances,
I was earth's spin and whorl to the pulls of stars,
I was magnet and metal. I had creation's spurt,
all time's fertility and blessing under my skirt......

16. Barlow young

Your Honour, she was Sarah's, Sally of Sarah,
Sally Salome, somebody's Sally, father
unknown. The evidence is a blather
of inconsistencies. I was a child. Doppelganger
barefoot, commando dressed, I slid the drainpipe
to Williams Street. I passed the poster.
Was it SALOME at the Alhambra?
Or was it MADELEINE NUDE doing her strip,

26

nakedly prancing at the Victoria?
Surely it matters. Creeping a daisied blackout.
I watched that wartime treachery abut
a chest of drawers, a broken radio,
a photograph in which five drunkards raised
anarchic fists at Blackpool Tower.
To the abundance of his pumping ardour,
the teardrop, peardrop cage rocked crazily. Its rod,
that chromium stanchion, shapes a question mark.
A spew of birdseed scattered to bequeath
fandangos on the buttocks beneath
a bouncing bird. Was that a cassock
disposed to hide his heretic betrayal
from a mirrored parrot, maybe budgerigar?

Coo-ee. Jacky's the name just as before
metamorphosed, mutated, transmutated,
colloidal, allotropic. Can you see me? Good.
That's me reflected in the spinning mirror
Somebody under me is seeding Sarah
in hairy heavings of adulterous doubt
where doppelgangers spin a double guilt
in the reflections of another mirror.

Or was it the blackout curtain the cage wore
on another night? In her orgasmic carol,
I heard her name him. But was it Simon
or Simeon I spoke in memory's subterfuge?
When Billy stood demobbed beside the cage,
was it *Ooooh Simon* or *Ooooh Simeon?*
Who was it spewed the instruments of Sarah's murder
he heard repeated to his bomb-burst ears?
Your Honour, the reliability of budgerigars'
(or parrots') cluttered tongues is little better
than the mess we make with our own. And what
did Billy believe? Your Honour, a voice
in one of its many variations….

17. Sarah Lucas

….*Ooooh Simeon,* I said. With Billy out of the way,
gone to the war, me urgent for Sim's passion,
peering beneath the window, juicy
with expectation, using Billy's reflection,
that foolish photograph beneath the Tower,
to be my lipstick's mirror. Sim used to like
rhyming our Eden grossness but I was all for
a taste of purple prose, so with my lipstick
I wrote SALOME BARE, scrawling it there
on a bit of newspaper, watching in Billy's window
his trousers swelling to lust's insignia.
I'd always fancied reading the canto
his trousers shielded, never believed
his lyric hypocrisies and virginities.
It was his poem SALOME BARE that charted
her dance and her undressing. I wrote its
title in lipstick to watch him learn.
my need. His stanzas moped the spirit but
soon he was searching me, draping the curtain
to shield the cage from flesh at flesh's trick,
baring his inspiration's swollen token,
polished for publication. Flesh is weak
but that stood strong for me. Passion
was all I felt when he began temptation's
stretching of ribbons to bulge my willing breasts
and his long mumble of nipples taut as bobbins
to grant his license. My body told him *Yes.*
I panted *No,* but unresisting offered
freedoms above my stockings, his urgencies
stretching my knickers. I whispered *No,* but ached
their soon safari past my knees. My thighs' pages
opened to learn his fingers' fiction
of licence's rhythms. My flesh said *fuck.*
My body's metric said *Yes.* My sucking Eden
of passion's breath said *Now.* But when I took
his swollen language for its limerick ride.

his iambic failed, sprawling stickiness to waste
on a taut suspender. Scutters of birdseed
dribbled the cage above us, shaping a dust
and frogspawn myth on disappointed thighs…

18. Barlow

…..it's CRASH…disgorging to light and scrutiny
that khaki cuckold beneath the Tower's rails.
How did he learn his Sarah's birdseed betrayals
beneath a chromium question mark? And could he,
supporting Babel's architectures, comprehend
what some voice told him? Was it the breeze
gibbering its bogus languages? Did those
cat's-cradle girders curdle the wind
to knowledge? Betrayed by innocence to laugh
with Sim and others near the ebb-tide's grammar,
still pissed and inarticulate for photograph
beneath the conundrum Tower…

19. Sarah Lucas

'Poor Simeon,' a parrot chirped.
She rasped her nails on the cage's wire.
'For Christ's sake, Jacky.' The shit-slug slipped
out of the frame. 'Simon,' it cheeped, 'poor
Simeon.' Truth's mirror ravaged her.
'You've dropped me in the shit,' she said.

20. Barlow

…it's CRASH…I'm wearing my budgie suit
but ready now to quit my question mark pretence
of cuttlebone and lies, and losing patience
with my capricious mirror. Somebody's appetite
is seeding Sally. Sally Salome and not Sarah,
Sally of Sarah. Whose urgent bum and back
wrestles between her thighs? Could it be Tom?

Or do I see my own in Billy's mirror?
Sally loves Tom. That legend's words
profane her lipstick forearm. Your Honour knows
that arse's owner. The only certainty is this:
a coital and delighted leg straining towards
a moment of orgasmic satisfaction
kicks Billy from his frame and on the back
of folded sheets of newspaper, in bloody lipstick,
someone has written SALOME BARE. And on
another surface, sanguine, somebody wrote
Coiled pipes and tripes. Surely Your Honour guesses
that there's untruth about, that someone's
been lying. Get me out of this bloody budgie suit:
let me re-shape my window-mirror's lies.
Dissolve that crap descent to Williams Street.
Balls to that drainpipe. I'm tired of sliding down it.
Shelve the posters, the MADELEINE NUDES, SALOMES,
all that I've lied about. That bloody budgerigar
never existed and I invented birdseed
dancing a heaving arse. I now intend
to change my evidence. Those tales of Sims were –
I made them up, concocted, shaped my squeak
to blabber parrot dreams. I didn't think…

21. Barlow

….it's CRASH….it's tantrum time. Someone's been lying.
She shoved me away and called me treacherous,
howled that she wanted Tom' caress
and smashed her father's photograph. Ready for playing
old octopus, ripe for the sticky thrum
of skin's wet engines, my cock drooped disillusion.
Pissed as a crab, she would not play. Someone,
she said, had played the parrot liar. Tantrum,
she raved her drool for Tom. I was not wanted.
A spider shinned the mirror where my offence
suffered her puny fists. She raged her Salome dance
had been for him and bared the lipstick legend

staining her arm. *Sally loves Tom*
And who was Jacky? Which was Jack?

She pushed me away
All this baloney
was Sally playing Salome.
She said: or could she say?

22. Sally Lucas

…..I danced a finer world than this. It was
a universe of butterflies and apples,
roses and rainbows. Its lovely language was
of flourishing and favouring, of succouring
and nourishing. I spun and spun. I was both long-
itude and latitude then. My little embrace
outstretched could hold the poles. I was all myths,
tranced by the teeming jazz of my ancient guts.

After the boozy kisses and gropes, this was,
moved in me, that command, like swallows when
they ride on thunder-thermals, as straight thunder-rain
crashes slack water to a living mail.
Dance, it said, dance. Came from a richer parable
of rainbows, butterflies, apples, roses.
I spun and spun and spinning gathered them in,
thread to my twisting bobbin. I was truth then.

Oh what a parish I danced for them. I danced
all nourishing, flourishing, succouring, favouring.
And then I woke to what I have always known: to this dung;
to the pop-eyed boozing faces, the sozzled lechers,
the grunt and fumble bastards of this world's affairs,
with all that rainbow region burst and exploded.
Oh, I was aching to go back. I had been the bride
of a resplendent country. I could have cried.

23. Billy Lucas.

'Who shat on Sarah?' Billy asked,
bending a bomb-burst ear. The budgie,
cocking its head said, 'Simon, Simeon, Jack.'
A ball of shit slurred Sarah's open eye
beneath a question mark. 'Poor Billy.'
'She doesn't give a shit now. Sarah's dead.'

24. Barlow young

Your Honour, barefoot, carrying my shoes, my face
blackened to doppelganger, I descend
a multiple, uncertain drainpipe. MADELEINE NUDE
salomes on the wall. I crawl ambiguous
daisigolds of Williams Street (its railings earlier
gone to the war) and there within
the mirror room of number seventeen
(or should it be fifteen?) a budgerigar
(maybe a parrot) in a teardrop, eardrop
(it might be peardrop) cage suspended on
a chromium, silver question mark of stanchion,
stutters a counterpoint of lies that drip
to a tiled hearth. Next to four wireless sets
in quadruple exposure, six drunkards shudder
Blackpool's three Towers. And there, Your Honour,
they are at it together. We call them Sim, I guess.
Sextuplicate and equidistant, equally
lit by the bright hearth's untruth, they are held.
In their left hands they grip a poem newly titled
by someone's lipstick. Sarah and Sally Salome
eye it intently. SALOME BARE. *'Coiled pipes*
and tripes,' they read, *'is all we are.'*
In sonorous and declamatory voices, Your Honour,
those are their words. Among them, a parrot is
staggering to counterpoint and seed-
less silence. Eyes sparkle applause and so,
septuplicate within a mirror-window, we know

32

collisions of doppelgangers, are dissolved
by a beginning and ending....

    Coo-ee, I'm here again, mercurial,
    kaleidoscopic, existential nark,
    I reign chameleon in a question mark,
    am concave, convex in a spinning mirror's tale.
    Someone connubial with my stanchion lies
    a carnal doggerel's ontologies.
    How did it happen?
    Your Honour, listen ...

                      ....Yes, Your Honour,
shit and derision, here I come, aged eight, clogs in
my hand, face blackened to commando (we intone)
crawling the outhouse roof and abseil, after
a fashion, the drainpipe to the backs.
MADELEINE NUDE *(we say) dancing a poster,*
flaps in the breeze. And innocence, Your Honour,
here dissolves....

Leeds. Liverpool Canal.

K Howden
'75.

Interlude

Frogspawn

I was lusting only for frogspawn there, Your Honour.
Still ponds were all I sought. This was in Eden
on its first apple day. Bluebells, I think,
were on the rampage: birds bustled in the banner
of rainbow light. The spring pools were green
with hanging trees and down ward grasses sunk
in mirror parishes better than ours, Your Honour.

In Eden, threshing among green fern, Your honour,
bashing among the bluebells, they were at it together,
that nearly naked possing on rainbow ground.
I saw them, playing young flesh's concertina
in a parish of butter flies. While I was there,
Adam gave Eve his gift of frogspawn and
regretted nothing. We call it love, Your Honour.

I was fishing only for roach that day, Your Honour.
They bite well on warm evenings. This was in Eden
that late, corrupted summer. Hayfields, I think,
spilt their milk ointment on the wind. Could there
have been an untimely cuckoo? Every reflection
told mirror parables of a perfection sunk
and lost beneath the rainbow scum, Your Honour.

On the long bankside, where the canal, Your Honour,
breeds rainbow grasses and swifts dip, feasting in air
I saw them quarrelling while swans thrust near.
It was his frogspawn lodging squamous within her
that she complained of. This Eden day, there were
no butterflies. The canal was a broken mirror
reflecting nothing. We call it love, Your Honour.

Enigma

1.

Swans threshed to join our quarrel
breached petrol's rainbows in fouled water.
Riding the air was the milk parable

of hay drying under the moor.
Scriptures of wind traced tissue scrawls,
ouija words on the landscape's mirror.

Each paddle's tear bulged to a churning
cosmos where ruptured surface raced to heal
the split scum's nerve. Shivering

fronds and diaphragms hid the mirror
of her discontent. A lost harmony struggled
to readjust the world's repair.

The stilled canal rebuilt the hanging
taint of our landscape. Air carried the screams
of feasting swifts to seal our ending.

2.

Yes, there were nettles and a light wind
walked in slippers on the water,
painting distortion on the constrained

and parcelled levels. Discontent arched
its back and two fat swans towed stripes
of bubbles, pulsing to our side

with all the shallow haughtiness
of self-importance, reared cup-handle throats
over the rainbow petrol's gloss.

And yes, a disenchantment gripped
my mood. His eyes implied a grace
I have never seen. A blown roach flopped.

Stirred water chewed the sun to slush
in a world turned upside down. And yes,
there were nettles. And after that, not much.

In Sim's Greenhouse

Sun gnawing in her earth rooms
bursts her brown belly apart. Mulch membrane
swells pneumatic. I mourn sometimes
for Billy underground. By now, the sun
digests him, past the ebb-tide's run.

See the tomatoes' bulging balls, their slings
of seed inflated tight as tyres. I yearn sometimes
for Sarah underground. Rich pickings
under her fronds, good compost for
time's trowel's thrust. The ebb-tide tumbles her.

Sun's groping fondles supine loams,
sinks his round muscle in warm tilth, shapes growth
with increase's command. I ache sometimes
for Sarah underground. She brought my root
from winter. The ebb-tide has no wait.

Cool water from the butt slakes the root tongue,
trembles muck's gut. I thirst sometimes
for Billy underground. Is there drink there? Young,
we roistered, sank slewed golds of ale.
He sups beyond the ebb-tide's fall.

From the *Bugle*

Present day moaning about England's lack of international success and dearth of goalkeeping talent brings forcibly to mind a lad who at one time seemed likely to become one of the greats of the game. The only reason for Sam Herod's failure to scale the heights and set the game alight for many a year was a broken leg which ended his short but outstanding career. He began with amateur sides but even as a youngster it was obvious to those who spotted his talent that he would shortly grace the higher leagues. One Manager at the time said that he had every skill – great athleticism, mobility, command of both goal-line and penalty area, timing and foresight – that a goalkeeper needed in the modern game. He started in Division Three but within a season was playing in the First Division. It was with City he came to the fore and progressed so quickly that within a couple of seasons he had made his name and jumped to prominence with the Inter-League and International sides. Everything seemed set for a magnificent career but tragedy struck when City were striving for the First Division Championship and his leg was broken. At first, the true seriousness of the injury was not recognised and it was thought he would be fit for the next season's fray but after several attempts at a comeback, it had to be recognised that he would never play again. City did their bit for him and he left the game with the proceeds of a number of benefit and testimonial games. He now keeps a hostelry in the area but in these days of goalkeeping dearth, I've heard his name mentioned more than once or twice and there can be no doubt that England's selectors would be glad to have a keeper as talented as their one time 'Golden Boy' between the sticks…

A Lipstick Concertina

1. Barlow

With her Salome dancing spent
in the Union Bar, Sally fell on her arse.
I fanned her with the Park Drive advert. Tom was
scumbling her drool, splaying the red taint
of lipstick over her face. I quit the bar.
Outside, the canal was a broken mirror
reflecting nothing. I was crucified there
by memories of that SALOME poster.
I was not barefoot then. But when I returned,
Herod was strutting pissed on the lighted stage
of his snooker room, drunk as a dog
and silently stroking balls about the arcade
of his table, crooning their measured movement
his birthday delight. He swore Sim his oldest friend,
regretting their quarrel, mourning a cue he'd
once broken in anger. Outside his spawning light,
Sally reeled with Tom She was well-oiled,
arseholed, Your Honour, absolutely pissed
and randy. She stroked my leg. Tom's fist
was parcelled, seeping bloody inside
a wrap of poster, dripping a lipstick spill
into a skin of sleet while Sally swelled
reciprocal to my fumble. *This bitch,* Tom said,
with her Salome buggerations - his hand's parcel
dripped lipstick – leaves all the fucking clearing up
to me. Snot, glass and broken bottles.
Look at my bloody hands.... Little roses
ripened to apples at his feet. A tied pup
howled misery up the night. Tom said,
My living's in my hands. You can look after her.
Sal minced to my side and coppelganger
voices came with her – SALOME, MADELEINE NUDE.
They promised me her lipsticked lust,

41

tits ripe and knees elastic for a spreading.
Then I remembered birdseed scattering
a heaving arse. My doppelganger thirst
roared for its jaunt between her thighs.

2. Barlow

....and how redeem or render Herod's confusion
at the vision Sally danced, shaking her tits,
squealing her Eden landscapes' benefits,
her itch for birdseed business under the stanchion
of chromium question mark? Your Honour,
Herod was staggering and gibbering,
flailing the butt-end of his cue. Blue fag-
smoke cirrused from him, sowing ash over
his baize's plain. His whelking eyes stared
at landscapes I could not see. He garbled Eden,
blabbered of butterflies and roses, rambled of rainbows and apples. Blind drunk, untainted
countries feasted his mind...

3. Sam Herod

Dance of the seven strips in here tonight
with that tart Sally twitching round my floor
waltzing the old Salome, shouting about
some *savouring* and *favouring* in the bar.
How did she get like that? *But her dreaming look*
was way outside the pictures in my book...

How did she get like that? Her daft ballet.
And bloody drunk. I thought she had more sense.
Rainbows, she shouts, and *butterflies,* some silly
vision of *roses* and *apples.* Is there a chance
she'd found a place outside our trouble?
But her dreaming look... No, it's not possible....

42

How did she get like that? Out there
shaking herself, pulling down her straps,
and heaving her clouts about to bare
her belly and nearly putting her tripes
on show. *Rainbows* and bloody *butterflies*
she was shouting. *But her dreaming face....*

How did she get like that? Somebody fanned
her face while she was garbling on
of *nourishing* and *flourishing*. It twitched my mind –
an envy that she'd reached a richer region
better than this. *Her dreaming look said so.*
Is there a place like that to know and go?

Barlow I saw, face white at my window, staring.
That Eden place she reached. Balls run clean
in boroughs of content, smooth canon
rhythms in Eden landscapes succouring
flourishes, nourishes, calmly roll delight.
Hers was a better landscape for skin's outfit.....

4. Barlow

I watched a Punch without Judy show's parade.
His box was a striped pavilion's masquerade
as a snooker table. Blue fag smoke reeled
around his drunken strategies. He staggered
cursing and miscuing, burning his baize
with falling fag-ash. He damned Sim's photograph
for fancied wrongs. His cue was a bludgeon staff
flailing at nothing and his indecent curses
told his world's bleakness. Your Honour, such phrases
remain unfortunately true. He spoke his lustful
yearnings for Sally's squelch, dreamed a new role
for her lipstick's tube. The balls in bundles
scattered the floor, rolled from his violence
beneath the table. He bawled that Sim had
employed his cue for murder. Then he cursed

the broken leg that killed his football chance,
citing both bloods he saw in Sally's lipstick.
Blind, anarchic countries devoured his sense.
His sozzled ravings of old enmities
told his corrupted landscapes. Such a sick
vision, Your Honour, often afflicts us
and such a pessimistic drunkenness
often affirms our world......

5. Sam Herod.

Jig of the seven...my birthday booze. That tart
Sally's big tits. Puts all her bleeding
machinery on show. I'd give her suckering
and slavering and fuckering. Tom got
the little tart all guess-what, Sim's little bastard.
Adulterer, I called him, shagging her under
a budgie cage with birdseed blathering his gear.
Then walking SINNER in that sandwich board
for Sarah. And killed that Abel. Balls batter,
bastards on baize. Sour highlights promise
nothing but GOLDEN BOY BREAKS LEG. No apples,
rainbows, butterflies for me. No butterflies tonight. Face at my window. Barlow outside.
Tonight he's painting Sally's furnitures
with his brush. Sim told me birdseed on his arse
and afterwards split my cue on that kid's head.
Confessed it to me. GOLDEN BOY BREAKS LEG.
Comes out of time not innocent to time
not innocent. All sodding suckering her rhyme.
And perishing. Waving that bloody rag
of poster. SALOME. *Don't call me adulterer*,
Sim said. *Don't say you weren't. You were.*
GOLDEN BOY BREAKS LEG. Billy goes to war
and Sim plays Conshie to get at Sarah. Sucker
and fucker. That Abel skulks his gutter.
In mine, a broken leg. Some other bugger...

6. Jack Barlow

I watched a Punch without Judy show.
His stage was level baize, blue fag-smoke
cirrused over, and Herod, the old miscreant, took
the role of lurching puppet-hero,
spreading old pleasures to a photograph of Sim.
Oh, he was staggering and smiling. miscuing, sowing
fag-ash over his table. His cue was a hosepipe flailing
and his whelking eyes were staring to a dream
of somewhere better than anything I knew.
Such looks are culpable. Your Honour, he squeezed
reds liquid as lipstick in droves around
his baize, hammering balls in bundles into
the cushions, laughed at his wild miscues
berserk on the cloth. He blew a kiss
to Sim, blabbered lovingly of Sal's butterflies
and apples, mixings their colours with the hues
of her dancing lipstick. Utterly drunk,
an illegal country feasted his mind. He bawled
of rainbows, muttered of roses and revelled
in Eden landscapes. Your Honour, I think
such happiness unlawful and such behaviour
endangers the sanity we encure...

7. What the visions said

I am the vision landscapes. I am the slopes
of Easter fells. I am spring's pulse.
I am light crystalline lacing the bulge
ridges, defying the sun. I am all landscapes
rich with unfulfillable promises.

I am stone villages in frost sunshine,
zebra and gold. I am moorland gilding
in Eden's glow, my skies brandishing
the burgeoning of a better sun.
I am the parishes of never that one

time were. I am the lost inns of friendship
in rainbow principalities, I am the cool,
sanded rooms. I am the world's first ale.
I spill the enchanted companionship
of fancies shaped in hope's misshape.

I am the world awake, light's butterfly
boroughs of content, kingfisher water under
visions of bridges. My cirrus skies are finer,
higher. I am dream kingdoms in a fly's eye
of once-upon-a- nothing. I am that day.

..

8. Barlow.

.....or did anarchic
landscapes devour him? Or were there
my double-breathing anagrams to smear
his snooker room's limelit acrostic?
As randy as myself for Sally's tripes,
my Punchinello echo raged his box and old
miasmas of Sim and Sarah intervened.
He yearned to fumble (imagining my gropes)
at Sally's tits. He ached to garden (as he
believed I would) the flowerbeds of smooth flesh
over her stocking-tops. He lusted to stretch
(as he believed I would) the elasticity
of urgent knickers past unresisting knees.
Your Honour (as he believed I would) he stood erect
to grunt and babble lechery's dialect
between her thighs. Or did my eyes
invent all this? Did wish-fulfilment interpose?
My eyes were deaf. Maybe my ears were blind.
And had it been for me that Sally danced?
Or was it Tom? Somewhere between us,
counterpoint lusts danced their fandangos,
cloying the air with smoke that blew both ways.

9. Barlow

Your Honour, perceptions belching to compose
the tongue's symbolic realms make little sense
and world pretending some syntactic sequence
bleats consequence on chaos. Rainbows
arch often double-dyed and butterflies
hide talons. Roses, the commonplace thing,
have thorns. Most apples are crabs. Such blundering
compactions. Did some acrostic cloud the glass?
Did Herod dream or curse? Did anarchic countries
succour or devour him? Did he solemnly
stroke balls to Eden pockets, or did he
madly miscue? Did GOLDEN BOY chastise
his vision or did Sally's *Eden look*
breach sweet horizons? Was it a drunken antic
or did he stroll serene and autocratic
in a resplendent paradise? In my book,
Your Honour, such rammel questions
remain obscure. Certainty garbles my lies.
Were there two speeches? No. No compromises.
His one warble with words wrangled a Woodbine's
cumulus and fell with fag-ash dropping
to foul his baize. How many versions
of unsaid acrobatics danced fandango tunes
on the tiddlywink of tip anointing
his cue's dithering sceptre? Innumerable
starving apocryphas licked indecent lips
and claimed inclusion at his speech's agapes.
Your Honour, as he reeled or danced, no single
utterance paddled his glad or slobbering vision.
What meanings fell with fag-ash to his baize
is anybody's guess. Both visions laid their siege
to words in counterpoint and competition
for his tongue's end. Your Honour, gob ordains
a muscle too inflexible for our comedy's
complex compactions, carting such lies
and labyrinths, the stinking rabbit warrens

and simultaneities of our thought…

Foxes

Golden Boy Breaks Leg

These were his apple parishes,
the acclaim Saturdays of each league match
in pastures of green innocence. It was
that season the Chronicle and the Dispatch
labelled him, *Young player to watch.*

These were the rainbow regions
of the ball's arch in air, the slick grease
of its clipped travel over grass plains.
That early Saturday of the season, the Express
bugled him, *Young man heading for success.*

These were the butterfly boroughs
of his frame's arrogance, taut muscles skilled
prancing, the nerved sinews' dandy poise.
That later Saturday of the season, the Herald
spread *Star in the Making,* to boast his world.

These were the rot rose countries
of artifice in a short, affluent reign.
That last Saturday of his seasons, the Empire News
blazed *Golden Boy Breaks Leg,* the lost acclaim
of petty splendour. He never played again.

Maybe a fox runs beside us,
rips from us the roses and rainbows of our delight,
bruises the apples, crushes the butterflies,
with malice fashions the pitches we inherit
in shoddy seasons where no headlines wait.

Piano Tom

Qualifications? That popinjay pen-pusher
meant to humiliate me. I almost showed
what I was capable of. In a split second's anger,
my hands twitched in my pockets. Then I felt sorry for
his ignorance. *Put pianist,* I said.

Could you teach music privately? I could
have awed him with my hands. I'm not prepared to use
my time and talent tutoring some kid.
Put pianist, I said. I could see he was afraid
and learning the sort of man I was.

You could give bus-conducting another stint.
My hands twitched to be shown. I held them inside
my coat, watching him tear some petty document
he'd tried to trap me in. By then he knew I wasn't
someone to trifle with. *Put pianist,* I said.

We could find you better shop-work than the last.
I didn't show my hands, stayed cold and aloof
used natural dignity to disguise disgust.
Then I grew angry with him. *Put pianist.*
He'd guessed what I was capable of.

Booth Six is where you should be. My hands lay
before him on the counter. His eyes grew wide
as I turned them with hypnotic grace to see
their radiance transfix him. He knew what I
might do with them. *Put pianist,* I said.

I've never seen a one-handed pianist before.
Then I remembered Sally dancing *Salome,*
the bottles she broke and trod in that career,
that sliver of glass going mad in my finger,
the suppuration that ate my hand from me.

There is a fox runs beside us and rips from us
the parishes of our pleasure and delight.
I held him the prisoner of my hypnosis.
Put pianist. He sat bemused and speechless.
By then, he knew the sort of man he'd met.

The Landlord's Birthday

1.

The midnight of my fiftieth birthday, snow
smoothed the fell. Roads wore chevrons
In the near sidings, cooling engines
cricked in frost. I set the frame
for snooker, built a baize meadow.
Where are they, the hiding regions
of content? What bus travels that dream?

That midnight of my fiftieth birthday, frost
ambushed the windows. Under glass,
past masters, cues unwithered, raised their faces
from time not innocent to time not innocent.
One image held me, greener, mirrored to test
my birthday. *Those rose and apple parishes*
I dreamed - what bus climbs that ascent?

Set balls waited. I broke them. They
cannoned their rhythms in baize countries,
moved weirdly there. Rainbows and roses
burgeoned in their kaleidoscope
and magic patternings. *Where are the butterfly*
boroughs? Some benign impress
rolled in them. *What bus run routes to hope?*

That midnight of my fiftieth birthday,
balls ranged in landscapes of no evil,
arched rainbow miracles in a dream revival.
Clean ciphers clicked and re-arranged
their patterns birthing a found fertility
for landscapes marking my festival
in apple parishes. *What bus chevrons that road?*

2.

There is a fox runs beside us. Once admit
some source of love or delight,
the jaw bites hard, rips at the meat,
the skin and bones of our delight.

Millgate
K Howden '75.

In Sim's greenhouse

This was my greenhouse. Membrane
and fruit of its earth room,
pneumatic, was once mine. Rat sun
of my rampant summer frame
spawned its intestines and
roots' lust musclings wrestled tilth
with increase's command.

Who strung this hare to tarzan
manouevres at the door's unlatch?
Parables of blood drawl Eden
histories where death's rigours etch
the dribbled mouth, the hung
and clouded eye. Light mottles
its suspension. Who strung

this hare breaching my calm?
Comes back to me, that broken face.
Memory sucks a child's scream
where there were fallen apples.
Who drags my murder home?
This was my greenhouse. Mulch
membrane of its earth room

was once mine. Now the sicknesses
of my exile seasons scrape
the allotment's rot. Rank grasses,
and blown infections grope
through broken panes. An impotent sun
wheedles my tilth with anarchies
of weed. What fox eats my garden?

Healings and Woundings

Healings and woundings

1. Sim

I wept at Sarah's grave, the boneyard
on the moor's shove. Wet Chapel
scraped the sky's unrest. A blackbird
clattered in privet. Not much stirred.
Rain hauled its shredding curtain on the fell.

Mean girders of terrace streets
buckled their insult on a swell of moor.
Something waited. A tied mongrel howled its
lust. That blackbird in stunted privets
anthemed rain's fabric dragging over.

Sun-bonneted, he pedalled a gilt career,
trundling on wet pavement's varnish.
Wheels buckled akimbo, his pedal-car
laid trails on rain's drying lacquer.
And I remembered my strength's parish.

It was a dream. My taunting voices
joined cloud clearing the fell's shoulder
and I moved clean again. My pain was
a birdsong's dying fall. The gutters' sluice
held only rain's messages. No more.

It was my first clean day.The bird's anthem
psalmed my assuage: the mongrel's anneal
shrived me. Guilt left with that dodgem
down the pavement's innocence. I hymn
the dog's psalm, that bird's canticle.

2. Herod

Walking to watch the holiday football
my world learned peace's shape. Washing twitched white
in wind-hauled sunshine, agile
over turned earth. In an old pedal-car, that kid,
sun-bonneted screwed towards me. A blackbird
praised the sun's rake from dusty privet.

Farms under the moor burnt golden
in benison air. The Chapel challenged slant
slates into a driven sky. The fell clanged clean.
Something waited. His voice, absorbed and tuneless,
grew apples for my morning: his car's wash
of paint squealed gilded through sun's ointment.

Slate roofs bloomed gold. That blackbird
psalmed air's jubilee. A windscreen
bulged liquid hymns to the sun as that kid

crabbed past me. Roses and butterflies
blew in his voice as he pedalled the poise
of gilded morning in a new light's reign.

Sun sparked greenhouses in the pens. Heads bent,
gardeners bowed the earth's renewal,
the year's fertility in the allotment
fringing the moor, my pleasure's parishes in
a blackbird's eye. This was my rainbow region,
the burgeon bonus of that holiday festival.

Walking to watch the holiday game
my world found friendship's patterns. *Golden boy,*
he said, *breaks leg.* I knew it time
to set those words outside my anger's parish.
That blackbird shouted sun. He laughed and my trash
pitches, my wasted seasons, dropped away.

3. Barlow

Your Honour, I came whistling out of the house
to meet a scrumming sky. Some senseless
blackbird psalmed the rain's rake in the pen.
Streetlamps spawned their blurred bastards in
parishes under the pavement's gloss.

Then, with a box on wheels, that kid
torpedoed my shin. *Something waited.*
He said, *Sinner,* Your Honour. I swear he said it.
I heard that blackbird strangle his note
as I touched the sun-bonnet masking his head.

It was a skull, Your Honour, a bloody skull
I touched. I heard that blackbird throttle
his psalm to silence. *Abel,* I heard.
I swear he said it. Your Honour, remembered
voices within the stone were howling Abel.

A tied dog shovelled its lust up the night.
That blackbird cawed. Your Honour, Eden's blight
was on me. Wind mauled the lamps, or else
the sky's machinery stilled. *Cain, Cain,* dead Abel's
spectre spewed its lipstick sleight.

Your Honour, it blackened every star.
Abel, I know he said. Or did he say? Or did I hear?
The crippled streets were screaming. The moor's back
was baying the rain's insistent ache.
He pushed away. I tasted nightmare.

From *The Bugle*

Workmen breaking down a dilapidated greenhouse in the Sidings Allotment behind the Unicorn Club the other day, made an interesting and unusual discovery. Mr George Herod said that when he began to pull away the door he found red lettering beneath the flaking whitewash and soon discovered that the legend painted across its boards had once read SINNER. Mrs Herod, who was present at the time, remembered it as part of a sandwich board which once used to be worn by a celebrated local character. Mr Herod suggested that the webbing that had once formed shoulder straps for the boards had been used as a hinge. Many years ago, so local stories have it and many of our pensioners might remember, a man wearing a mask to conceal his identity used to walk the streets every Saturday wearing those boards. No-one ever heard him speak. Each week he used to walk once through every street, speak to no-one and follow exactly the same route. It was generally believed that he was making some kind of undisclosed penance. Mrs Herod remembered that these Saturday events came to an end when there was an unpleasant incident near the Unicorn Club in which a small boy was badly hurt. Mr Herod holds a theory that the boy was actually killed and the whole matter in some way hushed up though everyone else I spoke to believed that he had been no more than injured. Nobody remembered, or perhaps never even knew the man's name though there was a general suspicion that he had been *somebody important* and hence the reason for Mr Herod's theory. Almost everyone believed that the man has been a Conscientious Objector during the war years and Mrs Herod remembered him as *a fine figure of a man with long, flowing hair*. Certainly, those boards and the man who once walked between them have a small place in local history. The greenhouse in which they were found has long been in a state of disrepair and at the moment, no-one is certain of its ownership, but it's certainly curious that the boards should turn up so near to the spot where the incident with the child took place and perhaps even more so if we believe Mr Herod's theory that they were put there deliberately to commemorate that violent incident of so many years ago….

A Stigmata Sonata

1. Barlow young

Your Honour, Abel says Hello. It is
our little jubilee. Tomatoes
swell mythologies. The sun bites
our Eden allotment. Lolloping hares
slide symphonies through summer grass.

2. Barlow

That business with the later SALOME poster –
where to begin, what to include, how to sift
truth from the mind's shenanigans. I was pissed.
Herod was pissed, playing his Punchinello snooker
in the Union Bar, Sally's dancing was finished.
The canal was a broken mirror and only
long after closing time was I crucified by
those memories of a poster that once furnished
the Unicorn wall. This was before the sleet.
There was the long reek of cabbages gone rotten
from the allotments.
                    No, I was not barefoot then.
Later, I was alone and barefoot, the night street
deserted about me. A lamp-post's intelligence
betrayed my treason of bare footsteps' patter
through recent snow.
                  But that comes later.
I saw the illumination's blaze divergence
from the Unicorn windows and Herod's gadarene
lurch around his snooker table. Sally was pissed,
her dancing done, standing with Tom. His fist
hung in the rags of a poster whose once burden
had been SALOME. Blood red as lipstick
dripped from a corner torn, inadequately
wrapping his parcelled hand. He held a bloody
and swollen fist towards me and - in that smack

peculiarly his own, I think he said –
Breaks all the glass this fucking Salome.
Glass in my hands.. Bleeding like buggery... .
More or less that. Great gobs of his blood
fell steadily from an errant corner
of poster, wounding the snow already rouge
from lipstick under his feet. Then a tied dog
howled up the night and Sally left him there
to come to my side. The drip of blood
obsessed him. He moaned persistently
and in a fit of petulance, *This bloody Salome,*
he said, blood dripping where he stood.
My hands my bloody living. Your Honour,
I think he implied that I should take her.
It hardly mattered that I had......

3. Barlow

And now that Abel business. I'm pretty certain
Your Honour knows the history of the case.
Barefoot but carrying clogs I trailed Sim's progress
with SINNER on his sandwich board when rain
gospelled his paint to bloody statement.
He lurched between. Was it, Your Honour,
raining? Or did I dream the stigmata
commas of footprints wounding damp pavement?
Parrot behind him, aping his laboured stride,
I trailed to bait him. *Sinner. Sinner. Sinner.*
Sometimes I won small change, caught the odd copper
tossed as encouragement, but on the parade
in question, maybe I jibed too near for sense.
Maybe his corns were bad or on that Eden day
I scraped the raw nerve of his shame, untimely
breaching the cabbage reek from the allotments.
The old rip went mad, let fly a coyote howl
to fracture the unforgiving rain.
That bludgeon cue he carried, legerdemain
reshaped to helicopter. Under its whirl,

Your Honour, Abel died. I saw the symmetry
of spoke-blur cudgel rise where innocent Abel,
clutch slipping on wet cobbles, caught its flail
and cracked beneath the blow Sim aimed for me.
Whose footprints skipped a damp stigmata?
Your Honour, dexterous and wary, I sold the stain
to Abel, saw the skull sever and gape to grin,
saw his brain boil and peep, a split tomato
of tripes and curd bubble its bloody juices
in rivulets between the carapaces
of shining cobbles.....

4. Children's voices

Jack was the one who started it,
Jack the little bastard.
It was Jack who ducked
and shouted 'Get fucked,'
and poor little Abel got plastered.

Jack was doing the shouting,
Jack invented the trick.
It was Jack's little pole
that poked SINNER's hole
but Abel got the stick.

Jack was doing the dancing,
Jack was jigging behind
But that was the winner
when Jack shouted SINNER
And poor little Abel got brained

5. Barlow

The mirror streets were slimy with sleet's skid
and soon I was bumping Sally in
that room where years before in Eden's frozen,
transgressive seconds, I hid outside,
eye squeezed on a blackout window to observe
Sim poss his Sarah. Scutters of birdseed
bucked on his bum and the cage tinkled
to rock the eternal question in a curve
of chromium stand. And there beside the wireless,
her father's photograph sentried with his arm
looping Sim's shoulder and behind them,
the Tower's babel, the ever-bashing waves
and sealed within its own transgressive second,
a background to that drunken friendliness,
within the snapshot pier's gothic arcades,
a couple kissing. It was then, ecstatic and
extending her delighted leg, my Sally-Sarah
drop-kicked her father's snapshot from its place,
to shatter on the floor. In that sarcophagus
was a thrice-folded piece of newspaper.
Somebody's lipstick had inscribed *Coiled pipes
and tripes is all we are.* Locked in its crease,
Sim smiled in newsprint where there was
a plug for MADELEINE NUDE whose nakedness
starred at the Victoria. And there beside
a broken mirror, near the wireless, half-across
the chromium cage, we played old octopus,
tying skin's knot on pleasure's little tide.
Her handbag, open crocodile near the hearth,
disgorged the golden cylinder of her lipstick.
There was a fly confused about the season, stuck
battering the bulb. And suddenly, a death
came howling home there in my memories of
the SALOME poster, Sim opening Sarah's page
beneath the swinging and seed-scattering cage.
Came with the cabbage reek still blowing off

the sour allotments, that predestined odour
of doppelgangers, that long myth's fear
invading me again...

6. Barlow young

Your Honour, Abel prattles and here comes
our greenhouse summer. A hare prances
to the sun's tambourine. Tomatoes
shout Eden's randiness, each bulbous
sling of seed a fertile universe.

7. A Distant, Ecclesiastic Voice

Can a tomato speak to us? Can inanimate or organic objects communicate with us? Of course, they do not TALK to us in the sense that we use that word at its loosest, for we are the possessors, for good or ill (and who is to question those eternal and surely ultimately benevolent purposes?) of language. Now, our language is linear. It moves along at one idea's breadth as we use it. It is without circumference....

8. Barlow
             .... but stuff a budgie,
am I my brother's keeper? My mind
here photographs bare footstep punctuation and
wet cobbles. What mark was on me then? The sky
was lead where Sim wheeled tortoise in
his anger between those boards whose wounded paint
bled to apocrypha. Whose gibbering taint
was aping behind him bawling *Ooooh Sim?*
Whose little stick drummed tattoos? What rapped
his SINNER boards? Whose stigmata stain?
Am I my brother's keeper? Ratchets of rain
came scatterwaul, Your Honour, when something snapped.
He whirled in his boards. My mind snapshots
their extending gyre. What mark was on the man?
He wrenched that torment cue from someone

and flailed its bludgeon weight in whistle clouts
on someone's head. My mind's camera
holds only negatives where stigmata commas
shape my evasion tango and Abel raises
a choirboy face for innocence's murder.
Mind photographs the cudgel, the mesmeric splatter
of hedgehog head. Am I my brother's keeper?

9. Barlow young

Your Honour, Abel was singing and we ran
through a tomato Eden. Heat shaped a fine
translucence. Later, I found the broken
sandwich boards shaping a greenhouse door,
a dead hare swinging its blood's parabola.

10. Barlow

Your Honour, Herod's poster MADELEINE NUDE
learned transubstantiation, bled to SINNER.
Can lipstick's transgression ever
re-shape the minds that witnessed that homicide,
that bludgeon's arc, that pulse of lipstick turds?
Who pushed? Who struck? Who fell? Not me, Your Honour.
I tell the lies of Abel's hedgehog splatter.
There were compulsive voices. When I saw those words
(I mean that poster, MADELEINE NUDE),
rain squelching paint to my drool remembrance
and lipstick accusation, my long innocence
rotted me. The reek of cabbages came pumped
from hedgehog-succouring allotments. A mongrel's
yelp was ululating loss into the void.
Your Honour, I feel guiltless. MADELEINE NUDE
I lipsticked (carefully) to SINNER. Why else reel
from Sally panting in a warm bed? Why else,
barefoot and frozen make that stigmata trek
over the cobbles' sleet? Why else use her lipstick?
Your Honour, there were doppelganger voices.

11. Barlow

Your Honour, stuff a budgerigar,
this was a mirror day when sleet
exploded wet grenades along the street.
Barefoot but carrying my clogs, my comma
footprints garbled stigmata *(God, what
pretentious stuff)* on cobbles, and there, serpent,
I trailed him, cavorted near his boards where paint
had drooled to shape his SINNER to a red blot
of nonsense. Some apple-knowledge moved me.
I rasped the naked nerve of his shame.
Ooooh Sim, I bawled and howled. *Ooooh Sim,*
I moaned, in my stigmata naming, shaped a copy
of dead Sarah's accent, aping her cries
when, skewered under the leaking budgie cage,
she yelled her orgasmic passion. My sortilege
exploded seed again to his arching arse:
again she panted beneath him as I re-told
the trickle of birdseed to his bum. Your Honour,
he knew I knew. Inside his bloodstain armour,
I named him. He roared his anger, wrestled
my broomstick from my hand (I think I never
confessed to this before) to flail it like a helicopter
and break my dance, unmyth the snake-possessor
of his most inward shame. Abel, less clever,
stayed for his blow. Brain bubbled. Lipstick spew
blubbered the gutter's sluice. Choirboy Abel
gathered my wage. In that stigmata battle,
Sim called me Cain. *He named me.* Told me he knew
my primal name. Where did he learn my mark?
Primordial on Eden's cobbles, slimy
as sodden leather, we lurched our destiny.
Doppelganger, he called me *Cain.* Is there a start
or ending to this blighted garden's dance?

12. Barlow

Confession time, Your Honour. I saw again
the bulge of forearm, the cue descending,
the commas of my naked footprints dancing
evasion's polka and that tormented man.
Your Honour, Abel staggered. His brains' lipstick
boiled on wet cobbles…
    …………but now, the poster.
I was warm and hard in Sally's bed, lust's pauper
ceremonies near completion when they came back,
those doppelganger voices, the rank smell
of cabbages, stone leaking mischief's audit.
I pushed and Abel fell….
    ……..all right, I've said it
at last. Discharge some of my purgatorial
residence. I heard again those voices –
Remember Abel dead. And oh, they were
insistent, Your Honour, telling me the poster
had to be changed. And so with Sally's
lipstick I'd filched, the transubstantiation
under discussion occurred. Beneath my fist,
among the reek of cabbages that pressed
and stone leaking insidious corruption,
that later SALOME changed to SINNER…
…………..all right, I've said it.
Is that enough? Can I expect a few less
of hell's abominations? The voices
ordered it. Dead Abel's memory enforced it.
Do I get fewer penance days? Can lipstick's splatter
unshape the past? Can guilt so comfortably
be lipsticked away? SALOME bled profusely,
SINNER was my remorse transfusion. Later,
I added drops of blood leaching the letters.
With such materials and suffering profound
personal discomfort from that saraband
of self-indulgence and small tactile pleasures
as yet unbrought to their spitting conclusion,

I think I made a passable job of it all.
Your Honour, can this confession curtail
my waiting limbo twitchings.....

13. Barlow young

Your Honour, Abel is dead. We run
no longer in Eden. In the greenhouse, a hare
swings bloody and broken. A long myth's fear
regathers. Flies batter for a sun
they cannot gain. Who made this garden?

14. A Distant, Ecclesiatic Voice

....It has long been understood by members of this fellowship that
inanimate or organic objects, even one so unlikely as a badly
stuffed hare may, under circumstances of special pressure, act as
storehouses of emotion engendered in their vicinity. That is to
say, should some violent or some strongly engendered emotional
action - let us say the killing of a child - take place within their
aura, it may be recorded and held, almost as a voice may be held
by recording it. Once so recorded, the act lies stored, awaiting
release when time and conditions are right. These recorded
emotions, like mushrooms when temperature, humidity and
season are propitious, may be released with great and compelling
force. Within this hare I feel ....

15. Barlow

...someone's been lying, Your Honour.
The streets were sodden and pooled, facades
of another day exploding sleet's grenades.
Her doppelganger promises raised me cocksure
to have her heaving under my lust
in that cold room where years before I had seen
the birdseed bounce of her begetting, that Eden
scoundrel at wartime's tricks. He possed
his Sarah beneath the swinging stanchion's question,

while over him the cage was dripping
my ambiguities...
        ... there, Your Honour, sitting
near a green frame, its wood and innards sown
with birdshit's lace, poised silly for snapshot,
his arm about Sim's shoulder, cuckolded Billy
grinned his long ignorance under the Tower's lie.
Your Honour, I still swear I can feel the waft
of a gull's wing...
                ....then it was tantrum time.
Angry, she shoved away my grope and called
me treacherous, howled out for Tom and smashed
that frame to the hearth where, vomit from
its gut shot sheets of cardboard, rotten
with budgie crap, and a thrice-folded gralloch
of newspaper. Staining its page with lipstick,
someone had written SELF-DISSOLVE and someone,
my doppelganger self, called from the past.
Erect to play old octopus and ripe
for the sticky journey of lust's trip,
my cock drooped disappointment. Pissed,
she would not play. She raved her drool
for Tom and not for me. A spider
shinned on the mirror while her anger
raised puny fists. She raged her Salome reel
had been for him and bared the lipstick legend
staining her arm. *Sally loves Tom.* Your Honour,
her tantrum soared. I quit...
                ....but later, on Herod's poster
I scrubbed out MADELEINE NUDE and
over that name and with the lipstick I took
from Sally's spawning handbag, scrawled
that message, SINNER. Your Honour I intended,
cipher to wound her for my drooping cock,
to remind and slight her....

16. Barlow

Coiled pipes and tripes is all we are.
A long intention rotted me with its pulse.
Why else should I leave her panting and why else,
Your Honour, steal that fistful of lipstick from her?
There were compulsive voices, Your Honour.
Your Honour, it's time to detail the case.
Exhibit One*: two children, a sodden road.*
Who struck? Who fell? Who knows what will intended
that hedgehog murder? Exhibit Two: *is*
the rain and somebody's maladroitness.
Your Honour, who slyly pushed? Who screaming fell?
Coiled pipes and tripes is all we are.
Blood crieth unto me. Am I my brother's keeper?
(Genesis four, verse eight*). Poor frogspawn Abel*
is Exhibit Three*,* spawning his lipstick's spill.

17. Barlow

....lamentations. But, Your Honour,
stuff a parrot, tape-deck I was there. My bones
recorded the deed and memory's distortions
replay it. Was I my brother's keeper
when bleating budgies of children gathered
to mock his caged indifference with SINNER
tomato on his boards? What doppelganger
is it that shouts *Ooooh Sim?* The tape jerks blurred
and indiscriminate. Sleet hisses illicit
siffles of budgie seed's adulterous dreams
to a wet street. Whose accent sways his halms?
My tape judders betrayals. In the near allotment,
cabbages reek where promiscuous tomatoes
swell pregnant worlds. Who bawls *Ooooh Sim?*
Is it a dancing child or is it Sarah's mime
preserved magnetic in the stone? Who knows?
The tape recording her orgasmic anthem
when Sim splashed into her urgent tripes is broken.

His bludgeon rose and fell. Was his intention
merely to scare? Did budgie voices blind him
or did my doppelganger accent lure?
Was it the birdseed hiss of rain? Maybe.
But none notches the tape. Blood crieth unto me.
Ooooh Sim. That howling perpetrator
rests unidentified. One child ducked the blow.
I saw the other fall. Your Honour, his head's juice
ran splashed tomato in the gutter's sluice.

18. Barlow

Your Honour, Exhibit Four: *Miasma. Abel's
small, staggering fall.* Came crawling from his head
his frogspawn secrets. A squashed tomato spawned
a lipstick myth. *Cain,* the voices called me. Coils
of pipes and tripes serpented on wet cobbles.

Your Honour, squelching frogspawn in Sally's bed,
my groping fingers searched an old compulsion,
found inculpation latent in her bone.
Abel lurked in her secrecies and shouted
Remember. Remember was all I did.

Your Honour, with her lipstick I ordained
Exhibit Five: *Coiled pipes and tripes is all
we are.* Or else, was SINNER my scrawl?
I know that while I traipsed that lipstick legend,
visions of a lost Eden pummelled my wind.

19. Barlow

Your Honour, because of his boards' red legend,
they called him SINNER. His name, I heard, was Sim.
I hardly knew him. I never knew him.
Mind's cinema pans an undulating land,
a veiling rain, a village cut from its parent scar,

some buckling outpost on a tyranny of moor.
Allotments smirk with bulge tomatoes where
SALOME is on offer at the Alhambra.
The camera *(cinema verite)* follows stigmata
commas of clogless feet dancing damp stones.
A cue rises and falls. Film in my Odeons
shows a stumbling child. Your Honour, they say
his name was Abel. I never knew him Something stirs
a technicolour memory, maybe it drizzles
and clogless footsteps dance wet cobbles.
A cue rises and falls. My Odeon flickers,
projects a howl – *Ooooh Sim* – but I don't know
this section of the film. It's realistic. The clips
show actors well-rehearsed and close-ups
clarify all. Anterior to the blow,
flailing at nothing, someone pushes Abel.
Close observation proves it. There is a shriek
animal in its terror, one not unlike
the death-cry of a hare. Now in slow-motion's fable,
a head batters the kerb. MADELEINE NUDE,
some week's performance at the Victoria,
wears flesh's monochrome where technicolour
ketchup is spattering. In memory mode,
the film is always breaking though the voices
often continue. Invisible in the screen,
still on the sound-track, a hare or someone
is shouting *Cain, Cain, Cain*....

Ross Mill
Britannia
Keith Howden 75

Some beginnings and endings

Barlow

…..with Sarah's daughter, Sally Sarah
begat (remember?) in some blackout deed
beneath a budgerigar when birdseed
trickled a bumping bum while Billy's laughter
under the varicose, meccano network
of Blackpool Tower watched his adulterous wife.
I thought Sim, doppelganger, was out of my life.
In the Union Bar, I met him bounding back,
his fist wrapped in a poster, MAD NUD its saga,
blood-bannering his hand. Doppelganger
passions lurched on a collision course. And stranger
voices. One howled *Ooooh Sim.* Another
remembered Abel dead. Sim stamped the bar
like a wet street. No sandwich boards bled
his SINNER legend, but emblazoning his hand,
he whirled MAD NUD. When I turned from Sally, there
clamouring to break the cold window,
dead Abel shrieked admittance. Your Honour,
I believed Sim gone, never again to blather
that blood day's killing business, even though
his memory has walked stigmata with me since.
He came again, his fist an incandescent flame,
MAD NUD a crumple on his hand. And with him,
dead Abel, insidious, to denounce
the tap-room with his remembered squeal.
Hands that had flailed a cue now wore instead
a burning poster. Its message was MAD NUD.
Punk priest of all my punctured days, dead Abel
spat blood into my face….

Back-Row Bulletins

1. The Globe

Your Honour, at the Globe I first
steamed for her swell. On the newsreel,
the *Graf Spee* scuttled. Weaponry raised,
assaulting cruisers fumbled buttons
of shellburst through a blue blouse. A sly
torpedo unzipped silk and slipped beneath
froth at her bows. Her engines shuddered.
Filaments of her rigging parted
over the blister turrets bulging
their stubby guns. One turbulent heave
shook all her structures and a tremulous
sucking signalled her gone. Close-ups came
of sweating faces looming, fingers
saluting air and that strange victory.

2.

Your Honour, at the Palace, stubborn
resistance crumbled. On the newsreel,
Monte Cassino fell. A clumsy
infantry pressed to open up the slopes
and hold the lower landscape's fabric.
Soft flanks gave way and reinforcement
of the encircling cordons stopped. Commandoes
scaled bare approaches. Opposition
slackened. A hot advance surrounded
covered emplacements hardly shielding
a deployed division. Unchallenged
shock troops reached their prize. A moaning
siren breathed its surrender. Close-ups
caught panting corporals embracing.

3. The Roxy

Your Honour, at the Roxy, I learned
victory's defeat. On the news, Russians
entered the *Reichstag*. The flags
came down. Supine the female city
disposed her limbs to that first column
hot to possess her. That military
ravishing by a crude soldiery
was mercenary stuff. No shining
citadel fell. She offered only
an indifferent body that bemoaned
lost politics and rued that enforced
nazi salute she harboured. How much
chocolate buys a girl? Close-ups framed
one blubbering her cheap dishonour.

4. The Court.

Your Honour, what am I doing here
alone in the Court? Why these newsreels
of *Nuremberg* trials? Can peace's
inquisitors in their other laws
weigh wartime's acts? All the evidence
is lies or vain exaggeration.
A Himmler chemistry and a Goering
swagger sits in the flesh. Our ether's
thick with a Goebel's propaganda.
I am myself. The lower ranks obeyed
blurred orders from a higher command.
Who shaped my state? A madman hiding
in an impregnable bunker. Close-up,
one familiar, unregenerate face.

The budding poet of the twentieth century

Your Honour, tell me the voices exist.
I hear them, I have always heard them. I
once thought myself the budding poet of
the twentieth century. I would have written
my landscapes rich and fortunate with apples
but the voices wavered and broke. I would
have written apples but the word came birdseed.

Your Honour, I thought dead Abel's voice:
some have his accent. But there are others. I
thought I had poems to drive the world mad.
I would have written my landscapes nourishing roses
but the crippled rows straddling this unwelcoming
upland howled different voices. I would
have written roses but the word came lipstick.

Your Honour, I thought your voice,
but you are silent, have never spoken. I
had wanted to write the kingfisher parishes
and friendship's inns. I would have written landscapes
favouring rainbows, but the bald fells
baying the rain's ache strangled my voices. I would
have written rainbows but stigmata came.

Your Honour, whose voice speaks through us?
Coiled pipes and tripes is all we seem. I would
have written the world awake. I would have written
my landscapes succouring butterflies, but the blood's
insistence tainted such voices. I would have written
butterflies but heard, coiled pipes and tripes
is all we are. Your Honour, are the voices real?

Sally Lucas

I walked a dangling world. Lamps bubbled
in underground parishes. Somewhere among privet,
    a late bird scraped and bustled.
Came to me like a warm wind's motion, spawning
through puff-ball dandelions. A long rose-reek
hauled from the wet allotments, dragging blank street
    to a rich tropic.

In cinder yards, a shunting engine whistled.
My hung land shuddered. The wet lamps' shiver
    moved apples pendant underground.
Came to me like the windless stiffening
of air among soft elderberry flounces. The sheen
of wet rows rocking in the rain's new mirror
    bred shining Eden.

Somewhere, I heard a voice. Something it called.
A tied dog howled the darkness, its singing bark
    rioting up the night.
Came to me agile as swallows riding
on thunder-thermals. Lamps swilling underfoot
grew sudden butterflies in the spawning, dark
    parable of street.

My lost lipstick stained the gutter, a spoiled
and dead thing there. Light bulging a windscreen
    bloomed rainbow for my pleasure.
Came as straight thunder-rain falls, clattering
slack water to a living mail. What could I say
but *Jubilate?* Had I not danced a minute's queen
    of a resplendent country?

Barlow Unbound.

Moved through me like the air
of birds expectant in a summer drought,
sensing a distant rain.

Clenched terraces relaxed their muscle. The house
sacrificed its breath. The yard's prison stone
spat sudden burgeon and I was loose.
I ran rejoicing at the rich riverside,
    a new world bursting my brain,
    where flattened weed
contorted slow tattoos on the water's ride.
Children were thundering my rainbow birth
in warm allotments where before had been
    bald gardens, battered earth.

Moved through me like a wind,
that sudden shifting spawning the upward rain
of pissbed parachutes in airless yards.

The moor sang to me as I climbed.
Marching wind moved my words to hymns. The bald fell
boomed anthems for my joy. Stone verbs drummed
bass through the valley's shed. Light psalmed and rang
    in the air's polished bowl.
    White washing swung
cantatas through my sun's reborn redeeming.
It was all sun. Like larks or recent butterflies,
I butted it, blessing its brilliant ball,
    bawling my new release.

Moved through me like that moment
presaging thunder when an airless calm
stiffens among soft elderberry flounces.

In the allotment at the canal side,
cleared paths for my renewal, polished dust panes.
In the greenhouse, pricks of bursting seed
stabbed to a spangling light, a warm air sucked
    roots from their winter. The sun's
    rough emery scraped
rust from my metal for seasons left corroded.
I knew the seed's throb, the root's song,
the apple's gorgeous energy as it thickens
    to an ecstatic burgeoning.

Moved through me agile as swifts
riding on thunder-thermals, as straight thunder-rain
crashes slack water to a living mail.

www.ingramcontent.com/pod-product-compliance
Lightning Source LLC
Chambersburg PA
CBHW071019040426
42443CB00007B/849

* 9 7 8 1 9 1 3 1 4 4 3 6 4 *